Merry Christmas!

D0338617

The Lesson
A Fable for Our Times

Carol Lynn Pearson

Illustrated by

Kathleen Peterson

GIBBS SMITH

TO ENRICH AND INSPIRE HUMANKIND

Salt Lake City │ Charleston │ Santa Fe │ Santa Barbara

for my grandchildren
Sarah and Sydney,
Christian and Taralyn,
Learners and teachers of Love
    C.L.P.

For Steve
    K.P.

22 21 20 19 18   18

Text copyright © 1998 by Carol Lynn Pearson
Illustration copyright © 1998 by Kathleen Peterson

Published by
Gibbs Smith, Publisher
P.O. Box 667
Layton, Utah 84041

Design by J. Scott Knudsen, Park City, Utah

Printed and bound in China

Library of Congress Cataloging-in-Publication Data
Pearson, Carol Lynn.
    The lesson: a fable for our times/Carol Lynn Pearson:
illustrated by Kathleen Peterson.—1st ed.
        p. cm.
    ISBN 10: 0-87905-862-5   ISBN 13: 978-0-87905-862-3
    I. Peterson, Kathleen B., 1951-   II. Title.
PS3566.E227S68   1998
813' .54—dc21   98-4353
                                        CIP

On Robert's first day at school, he
had a wonderful time.
He swung on the swings.
He sang with the other children.
He listened to the stories.
He loved sitting at a desk and
smelling new paper and touching
new pencils. And his teacher was
very, very nice.

One day Robert's teacher said, "Children,
it's time for our lesson.
We are now going to learn how to solve a problem.
One plus one equals what?"

Robert was very curious and listened carefully
while the teacher explained.
Then he raised his hand and said, "The answer is two!"

"Right!" said the teacher.

And Robert was very happy
because he had solved the problem.

The next day when the teacher started talking about
solving a problem, Robert just stared out the window
at a bird that was hopping on a nearby branch,
because he already knew how to solve a problem.
But when his eyes went to the blackboard after the
bird flew away, he saw written there "2 + 2."

"What?" Robert looked at his teacher in surprise.
"Another problem?"

"Oh, Robert," the teacher said, twinkling as if she
knew some marvelous secret, "this is just the beginning.
There are lots and lots of problems."

Robert sighed. Then he listened as the teacher
explained, and he raised his hand and said, "four!"

"Right!" said the teacher.

And Robert smiled because he had solved two problems.

Every day when Robert went to school,
there were more and more problems to solve.
And sometimes Robert said to himself,
"This is not fun!"

But his teacher told him he had to
do it anyway, because what he was there
for was to learn. And he could have fun at
recess and lots of fun after school.
And she said, though Robert did not believe
her, that after he had solved lots of
problems he would feel even happier than
when he slid down the slippery slide.

So one by one Robert solved the problems.
And after he solved them he smiled.

And he moved up a grade.

Then one day the teacher said,
"We are now going to do story problems."

"Oh, boy," said Robert, "this sounds like fun!"
He liked stories,
so he listened carefully.

"If you are outside playing,"
said the teacher, "and you have three cars
and one truck and Joey comes along
and grabs two cars and the truck,
how many times should you hit Joey?"

Robert thought and thought.
"Two times!" he said.

"Wrong," said the teacher.

"Three times!" said Robert.

"Wrong," said the teacher, and she looked
at him with soft, expectant eyes.

Robert puzzled over this for a little while,
then his hand shot up and he said brightly,
"I know! No times!"

"Right!" said the teacher.

And Robert smiled because
he had solved another problem.

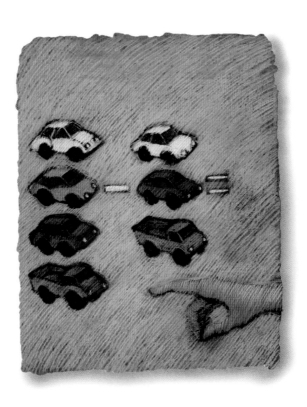

Robert grew bigger and bigger
and so did his problems. Oh, he loved
recess, and he played ball and roller-
skated with friends after school
and had the best time!
And the teacher saw to it
that they sang and drew pictures
and had lots of fun in class.

But always there came the problems.

And sometimes he slumped down at his
desk and said, "I am not enjoying this!
Why are you punishing me with all
these problems?"

And Robert's teacher, now twinkling as
if the secret were even more
wonderful, answered, "Oh, Robert, I am
not punishing you. It's just that you
have moved up a grade and are ready
for harder problems.
And here comes one now."

Robert held onto his desk with both
hands and squeezed his eyes shut
and listened.

"Robert, if you ride your bicycle
two blocks east and three blocks
north, and you fall off and break
one leg, is it your fault or the
bicycle's fault or the sidewalk's
fault or your parents' fault
because they gave you the
bicycle for your birthday last
August? And do you ever ride a
bicycle again, and what do you
do while you are lying in bed
and can't go out to play?"

Robert worked on that one for a
long time, and it was not fun at
all, but finally he got it right,
and his teacher smiled.

Robert was proud of himself
and he smiled too.

And the teacher moved him
up another grade.

One day as Robert was gazing out
the window at the raindrops that were
making puddles on the sidewalk,
and thinking what a great splash he
could make, he heard his teacher say,
"Robert, if your family moved to a small
house in a big city and you had to leave
behind two aquariums and one dog and
your best friend . . ."

"Oh, no!" interrupted Robert.
"I don't want *that* problem.
Give me a different problem!"

"But I can't," said the teacher. "This is
your problem and you must solve it."

So Robert worked on it and cried a
little, and finally, after some time had
passed, he found that he had solved
the problem. And he smiled.
And it felt good.

And the teacher moved him
up another grade.

Robert had a long summer vacation and
played and played and played.
And when it was time to go back
to school, he was ready.

For a while Robert was given some very
simple problems, like, "Robert, if you take
five minutes longer in the shower and
four minutes longer on breakfast,
how long will it take you to walk to
school because the bus already left?"

But one day Robert could hardly breathe
as he heard the teacher say,
"Robert, if you were a teenager
and you were not doing well in school
and you were not popular
and you had pimples all over your face
and your parents were getting a divorce
and you thought it must be your fault
and you felt that life was the pits,
would you
(a) take drugs to make the pain go away,
(b) kill yourself, (c) hate your father, or
(d) think of another solution?"

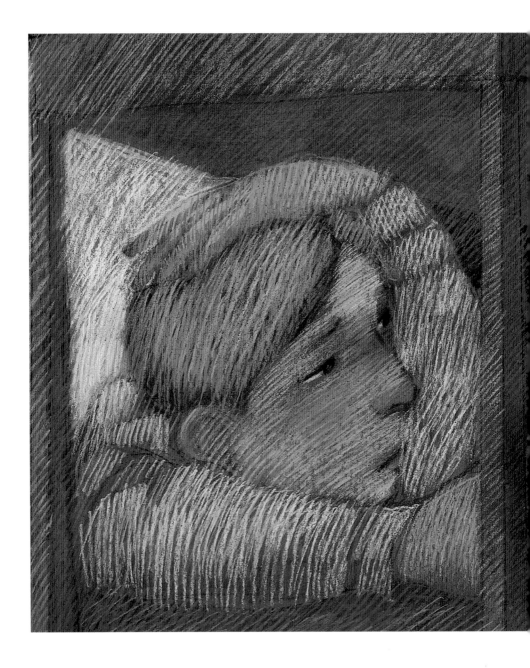

"Oh, no," said Robert, hiding under his desk. "I can't do that one! I like the problems about oranges and bananas in the grocery store or missing the bus. This one is too hard! Why are you punishing me?"

"I'm sorry, Robert," said the teacher kindly. "You're a big boy now and you have big-boy problems. Now come out from under that desk and solve it. You are here to learn."

So Robert slowly came out and studied
the problem and frowned and even
dropped a few tears onto his wooden desk.
He didn't get it right the first time, but
the teacher was patient and saw to it
that Robert had some extra-loving
attention. And at last Robert leaned back
and said, "Whew! That was a tough one."

"It was indeed, Robert," said the teacher.
"But you solved it and I'm proud of you."

Robert had thought he might never smile
again, but finally he did smile.
And on the way home from school he
noticed that the sky was bluer than he
ever remembered seeing it.

And he moved up to the next grade.

Robert's teacher gave him all kinds of
problems, and he eventually learned it
was no use to hide under his desk
or to tell her no or to yell.
They were *his* problems and he
would have to solve them.
And sometimes a new one came
before the last one was finished.
There was recess, and there were
weekends, and there were long holidays.
But always the bell would ring and
there was his teacher with a new
problem. And as soon as he got it
solved—you guessed it—
he was moved up to the next grade.

And it felt good.

"Robert, if you had seven dates with
one girl and fell in love with her and
four months later asked her to marry you
and she said no and you felt like
a complete zero . . ."

"Robert, if you really wanted to go to
college and it cost five thousand dollars
and you only had two thousand . . ."

"Robert, if your wife, who was really
a very good woman, had ten habits
that drove you absolutely crazy and was
thirty pounds overweight and spent
half her time on things that were
important to her but not to you . . ."

"Robert, if you had three children and one of them was born with a birth defect that added to your sorrows because it subtracted from her possibilities and divided your attention and multiplied the problems of caring for your family . . ."

"Robert, if you knew that your boss at work was cheating forty-five people in seven states in twelve different ways, and if you said anything there would be a ninety-percent chance you would lose the best job you'd ever had . . ."

"Robert, if you woke up fourteen mornings in a row wondering if it were worth it to get out of bed because you felt like you'd been giving one hundred percent to two dozen people and getting only thirty percent in return and you felt yourself going down and down and down and your brother's house went up in flames and your wife's mother was in a terrible accident and your daughter wanted to marry a jerk and the pollution thickened and the ozone thinned . . ."

Robert sat at his desk for years and years
and did his best. And everyone who loved him
gathered around and encouraged him,
but they knew they could not do Robert's
homework for him, for these were *his* problems.
And they each had problems of their own, and
Robert encouraged them, but the only
problems he could really work on were his.

And when he couldn't solve a problem,
no matter how he tried, the teacher was
very patient and smiled and said,
"That's all right, Robert. We'll come back to
that one some other time."

Gradually Robert stopped saying, "Oh, why are
you punishing me with all these problems?"
for he knew he was there to learn,
and he learned that learning made him happy,
and he found that he smiled a lot.

And he moved up from one grade to the next.

One day when Robert was a very old man and sometimes dozed off in the classroom, the teacher startled him by saying, "Robert, if your body had three heart attacks and one missing kidney and you got weaker and weaker until you could hardly breathe, how much would you have loved and who would remember you after you were gone?"

Robert swallowed hard and sat up straight at his desk and worked on it.

Suddenly he realized that all the lessons he had been learning all his life had really been only one lesson, that all the problems he had been working on all his life had really been only one problem—
this problem:
"Robert, how much do you love?"

Finally he leaned back and sighed and smiled.

And the teacher smiled.

And Robert moved up to the next grade.